ASK THE
CONSTITUTION

Do Women Have Equal Rights?

Elizabeth Schmermund

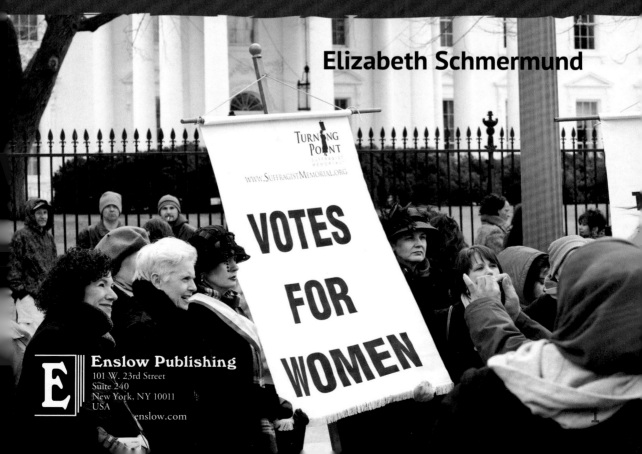

TURNING POINT
SUFFRAGIST
MEMORIAL
WWW.SUFFRAGISTMEMORIAL.ORG

VOTES FOR WOMEN

E **Enslow Publishing**
101 W. 23rd Street
Suite 240
New York, NY 10011
USA
enslow.com

Published in 2020 by Enslow Publishing, LLC
101 W. 23rd Street, Suite 240, New York, NY 10011

Library of Congress Cataloging-in-Publication Data

Names: Schmermund, Elizabeth, author.
Title: Do women have equal rights? / Elizabeth Schmermund.
Description: New York : Enslow Publishing, 2020. | Series: Ask the constitution | Includes bibliographical references and index. | Audience: Grade 5 to 8.
Identifiers: LCCN 2018052172| ISBN 9781978507098 (library bound) | ISBN 9781978508453 (pbk.)
Subjects: LCSH: Women's rights—United States—Juvenile literature. | Women—Legal status, laws, etc.—United States—Juvenile literature. | Equal rights amendments—United States—Juvenile literature. | Women—United States—History—Juvenile literature.
Classification: LCC HQ1236.5.U6 S345 2020 | DDC 323.3/40973—dc23
LC record available at https://lccn.loc.gov/2018052172

Printed in the United States of America

To Our Readers: We have done our best to make sure all website addresses in this book were active and appropriate when we went to press. However, the author and the publisher have no control over and assume no liability for the material available on those websites or on any websites they may link to. Any comments or suggestions can be sent by email to customerservice@enslow.com.

Photo Credits: Cover and p. 1 top, interior pages background (Constitution) Jack R Perry Photography/Shutterstock.com, cover, p. 1 Nicholas Kamm/AFP/Getty Images; p. 7 Bev Grant/Archive Photos/Getty Images; pp. 9, 31 Bettmann/Getty Images; pp. 10, 21 Everett Historical/Shutterstock.com; p. 15 Print Collector/Hulton Fine Art Collection/Getty Images; pp. 16, 18, 22, 25, 28, 29 Library of Congress Prints and Photographs Division; p. 35 Wally McNamee/Corbis Historical/Getty Images; p. 36 Mark Wilson/Getty Images; p. 39 Mario Tama/Getty Images; cover, interior pages (paper scroll) Andrey_Kuzmin/Shutterstock.com.

Contents

Introduction

In the National Archives Museum in Washington, DC, a yellowing document is encased in bulletproof glass and gold frames. The handwritten words on the page are hard to read, except for a large looping script that reads "We the People." This is the founding document of the United States of America, the Constitution.

But throughout the history of the United States, many women have questioned whether they are included within "We the People." Women were not allowed to vote when the Constitution was written. For many years, women were not permitted to own property or have the final say in whom they would marry. Until the 1970s, girls often had no sports teams to play on in school. There were no protections for women against stalking or to prevent women from being discriminated against while at their jobs. Even today, women earn less than men, on average, at the same jobs. One out of three women will experience sexual violence in their lifetimes—a much higher number than men.[1]

The Founding Fathers purposefully did not use the words "men" or "women" in the US Constitution. They used the words "people" and "persons." This was intended as a gender-neutral way of giving equal rights to all people. However, history has shown us that women have not always been granted the same rights as men. Women have had to fight to be included in the Constitution—most notably, to earn the right to vote. Because of this, feminist advocates argue that women's rights need to be added to the US Constitution, specifically in an amendment called the Equal Rights Amendment (ERA).

Amendments are laws or rules that are added to the Constitution to change it in some way. Through the years, amendments have been added, many to specifically and clearly address the rights of women and people of color. These rights include personal freedom, property rights, and the ability to vote. The first ten amendments are known together as the Bill of Rights. There are twenty-seven amendments to the US Constitution, with the first one being added in 1791 and the last in 1992.[2]

The Nineteenth Amendment, which we'll explore in detail later, was passed on August 18, 1920, and stated that every citizen could vote and that voting could not be denied based on someone's gender. The Equal Rights Amendment, which we'll also explore in this book, has still never been fully passed by the states.

This system of amendments is different with the US Constitution than with any other constitution. Rather than completely changing or updating the language of the Constitution, amendments can only be added to the original document. What this means is that the original text of the Constitution remains incredibly important and cannot be changed. It also means that, since the text is somewhat short and was written hundreds of years ago, it is open to a lot of interpretation.

The idea of interpretation has proven to be a complicated issue—especially for issues regarding women. Do women have equal rights? If not, should the ERA become the newest amendment to our Constitution? But before we answer these questions, let's first find out what the Constitution says and how our federal and state governments have chosen to interpret it.

1

The Creation of the Constitution

I t's sometimes easy to forget that the US Constitution is a document that was created by a group of men with differing opinions. There were some disagreements over what would be included and what would be excluded from the Constitution. The Constitution is also a historical document, which means it was written during a particular time period and reflects the priorities of that time period.

The US Constitution was first written in 1787 but was based largely on the earlier Articles of Confederation. The Articles of Confederation was the first official constitution of the United States, written at the beginning of the Revolutionary War.

During the early years of the United States, politicians realized there was a need for a stronger central, or federal, government. On May 25, 1787, the Constitutional Convention began and seventy-four delegates from twelve states were named as contributing to the Constitution. Thirty-nine delegates signed.[1]

Not everyone was happy with the US Constitution; some delegates left, while others refused to sign. Benjamin Franklin stood up on the final day of the convention with a prepared speech in his hand. He stated: "There are

Women have marched for their liberation since the early 1900s. Here, the Women's Liberation Movement unites with the Black Panther Party to ensure rights for the oppressed in the 1960s.

several parts of this Constitution which I do not at present approve, but I am not sure I shall never approve them … Sir, I agree to this Constitution with all its faults, if they are such; because I think a general Government necessary for us."[2]

For the Founding Fathers, however imperfect the Constitution was, it was a necessary step toward a government founded for the people and by the people.

Whose Constitution Anyway?

The finished document also drew inspiration from Enlightenment thinkers like John Locke and Edmund Burke. Enlightenment thinkers believed in establishing a government by votes, or by the will of the people. They believed it was essential that citizens voted of their own free will and with a free mind.

Because of this, it was thought that men without property, such as those kept as slaves, couldn't vote because they could be coerced into voting in the way their landlord, or "master," wanted them to vote. This was also one of the reasons why women were explicitly left out of the Constitution. Many Founding Fathers believed that since women did not own property and were typically subject to their husbands, they would not vote freely.

White, male landowners were the primary beneficiaries of Constitutional rights. African Americans, women, and those who did not own property were not ensured the right to vote in the original Constitution.

Mercy Otis Warren

Mercy Otis Warren was born in what is today Massachusetts in 1728. Prior to the beginning of the American Revolution in 1775, Warren was very active in the independence movement against Britain. Her writings about American independence and what a new American government should look like greatly influenced the Founding Fathers. Ironically, she herself did not want to see the Constitution ratified. In 1788, she published a pamphlet titled *Observations on the New Constitution*, in which she expressed what she felt were the faults of the document, including the large powers the new federal government would have.

Founding Fathers—and Mothers

There was a lot of debate during the Constitutional Convention about what rights should be included in what was surely to be the most important document of the new nation. None of the delegates were women. But this doesn't mean that some women didn't shape the drafting of the Constitution as well.

Mercy Otis Warren was a well-educated woman who lived in Massachusetts. She married a legislator and, through him, became known to many other politicians of the day. She would exchange letters with George Washington, Benjamin Franklin, John Adams, Thomas Jefferson, and others. During these exchanges, she would give her readings of important Enlightenment ideas and offer opinions on how the new government should be set up. Although she was not legally allowed to be present at the Convention, her ideas were enshrined in the founding documents of the United States themselves. Warren wrote the now famous lines "man is born free and

Mercy Otis Warren was not legally allowed to attend the Constitutional Convention given she was a woman, but her words are included in the Declaration of Independence even so.

Men drafted the Constitution of the United States, but women like Abigail Adams advocated that women not be entirely forgotten during its creation.

possessed of certain unalienable rights."[3] These exact words are included in the Declaration of Independence, and their basic idea is enshrined in the Constitution.

Another woman who shaped the Constitution was Abigail Adams. She was married to John Adams, who would become the second president of the United States. Abigail Adams was a prolific letter writer and another well-educated woman. Adams did not believe that she could—or should—directly contribute to such matters as the forming of the new US government. But she did try to influence her husband in other ways. For example, she wrote:

"In the new code of laws which I suppose it will be necessary for you to make, I desire you would remember the ladies and be more generous and favorable to them than your ancestors. Do not put some unlimited power into the hands of the husbands. Remember, all men would be tyrants if they could. If particular care and attention is not paid to the ladies, we are determined to foment a rebellion, and will not hold ourselves bound by any laws in which we have no voice, or representation."[4]

Adams was well aware that power in the hands of only a concentrated few could lead to corruption or intolerance of others. However, her plea would go unrealized for nearly one hundred and fifty years.

Coverture

One of the main laws that kept women under the control of their husbands emerged from early European law. Against Abigail Adams's wishes, it became a part of early American law, too.

"Coverture" was an English legal principle that did not recognize a married woman as her own person. Once a woman entered into marriage with a man, she gave up many of her legal rights to her husband. In the years after the Constitutional Convention, "Dower Rights" were increasingly forgotten. These rights were given to widowed women and allowed them to own their deceased's husband's property.

With these rights often forgotten, widows were left in a tough spot financially. Some states began to realize that this could not continue in the 1840s. They began to pass laws that women should have the right to own some property. But this was a slow process. Some states would confer some rights onto women, whereas others would not. Advocates realized that there would need to be a federal law that would protect women's rights. But that seemed to be a long way off still.

2

The Early Women's Rights Movement

For many years, American women fought for the right to vote. The women who first began an organized fight for women's suffrage would not live to see the Nineteenth Amendment ratified in 1920. The United States was not the only nation that would revise its laws to incorporate women: the United Kingdom (UK) gave women the right to vote in 1928, while women in France voted for the first time in 1945.

Feminist Voices

Like the Constitution itself, laws that gave women more equal rights drew inspiration from previous thinkers. In the late eighteenth century, Mary Wollstonecraft wrote one of the earliest texts on feminism and women's equal rights. The book, *A Vindication of the Rights of Woman*, published in 1792, focused on how women were constructed to be inferior to men in England. She argued that women, due to their roles as caretakers and educators, had important roles in society and deserved an equal status under English law.

In 1837, the American abolitionist and suffragist Sarah Grimké penned *Letters on the Equality of the Sexes and the Condition of Woman*. In it, she explored the different roles that men and women played—men often played important roles in public life, while women were bound to the home. She argued that women had the aptitude—and should have the legal rights—to participate in work and politics and, especially, to do advocacy work for such relevant issues as abolitionism.

Abolitionists and Suffragists

The women's suffrage movement largely developed with and from abolitionism, the movement to end slavery. During the mid-nineteenth century, the nation grappled with the morality of the institution of slavery. Southern states wanted slavery to continue, while Northern states wanted slavery to be abolished.

Many Northerners wrote about the immorality of slavery and the horrors that slaves lived through. Frederick Douglass, an escaped slave who wrote his autobiography and became an advocate for both abolition and women's rights, shared horrors he lived through while a slave in the border state of Maryland. He would later speak around the country for women's suffrage. He stated:

"When a great truth once gets abroad in the world, no power on earth can imprison it, or prescribe its limits, or suppress it. … Such a truth is woman's right to equal liberty with man. She was born with it. It was hers before she comprehended it. It is inscribed upon all the powers and faculties of her soul, and no custom, law, or usage can ever destroy it."[1]

William Lloyd Garrison was also a vocal abolitionist and the editor of the *Liberator*. In this newspaper, Garrison published Sarah Grimké's *Letters on the Equality of the Sexes and Condition of Woman*, as well as her sister Angelina's works on women's rights. The newspaper became a platform not only for the immediate abolition of slavery but also for increasing rights for women.

Mary Wollstonecraft was an early feminist whose own daughter (Mary Shelley) would go on to write *Frankenstein*.

Sojourner Truth spoke about women's rights and how gender and race cause people to be treated differently from the standard set by and for white men.

For activists like Garrison, Grimké, Douglass, and others, women's rights and the end of slavery were similar battles to be fought. As Garrison stated, "Wherever there is a human being, I see God-given rights inherent in that being, whatever may be the sex or complexion."[2] Garrison and others wanted these "God-given rights" to be expressed in the legal documents of the United States—and especially the Constitution.

The Declaration of Sentiments

The women's suffrage movement would gain more steam with the first women's rights convention at Seneca Falls, New York, in 1848. Known as the Seneca Falls Convention, this meeting was organized by Elizabeth Cady Stanton, Lucretia Mott, Martha Coffin Wright, and others. Approximately three hundred people attended the convention—and Frederick Douglass was the sole African American attendee.[3] At the end of the two-day conference, the attendees had written and signed a document known as the Declaration of Sentiments, which was modeled after the Declaration of

Ain't I a Woman?

Sojourner Truth was born into slavery. She later escaped and became involved in the growing abolition and women's rights movements. In 1851, Truth gave a powerful speech, called "Ain't I a Woman?," speaking about the ways in which her rights had been denied because she was both African American and a woman.[4]

Sojourner Truth spoke about what we would later call intersectionality, or the way race and gender interconnect and cause people to be treated differently under the law. She also would speak out about the evils of both sexism and racism—and both were, unfortunately, present in the early women's rights movement.

Frederick Douglass agreed that women should have equal rights, but he also felt that black men should have equal rights—and the right to vote—before women.

Independence. Douglass called it "the grand movement for attaining the civil, social, political, and religious rights of women."[5] The document stated:

"We hold these truths to be self-evident: that all men and women are created equal; that they are endowed by their Creator with certain inalienable rights; that among these are life, liberty, and the pursuit of happiness; that to secure these rights governments are instituted, deriving their just powers from the consent of the governed. Whenever any form of Government becomes destructive of these ends, it is the right of those who suffer from it to refuse allegiance to it, and to insist upon the institution of a new government."[6]

The Declaration of Independence was written by the Founding Fathers, who stated why their "unalienable" rights were being ignored by the British Government and, therefore, why they would declare independence from that unjust governance.

Similarly, in the Declaration of Sentiments, women declared their suffering from the unjust laws that governed them and did not allow them a say in their political governance. They, too, declared the right to independence from such unjust laws. These were fighting words. Women's rights advocates would not rest until an amendment was passed that would grant women the right to vote.

3

Amendments to the Constitution

The Civil War came to a close in 1865, with the North declaring victory over the Southern states. The first amendment that was passed after the war in that same year was the Thirteenth Amendment, which abolished slavery across the United States. The Fourteenth Amendment, ratified the next year, would broaden the definition for citizenship in the United States, which had formerly excluded African Americans and former slaves. But it also introduced the first mention of "male" citizens into the Constitution, restricting the right to vote to males twenty-one years of age and older.

This brought a new set of challenges to women's rights advocates; previously, it was state laws that restricted the women's right to votes. Now it was the federal government. Elizabeth Cady Stanton wrote, "If that word 'male' be inserted, it will take us a century at least to get it out."[1] But it was the passage of the Fifteenth Amendment that would introduce even more turmoil into the women's suffrage movement.

A Nation Torn Asunder

The women's suffrage movement was largely halted during the Civil War, between 1861 and 1865. Before the war, abolitionists and women's rights

Susan B. Anthony was an early supporter of women's rights—especially the right to vote. To this day, women place "I Voted" stickers on her tombstone.

Elizabeth Cady Stanton (*pictured here*) spoke out against the passage of the Fifteenth Amendment. She worried that with all men given the vote, women would be forgotten.

advocates had worked together. After the war, however, a division among women's rights advocates emerged.

Some women, like Elizabeth Cady Stanton and Susan B. Anthony, wanted to fight for universal suffrage. They wanted the next amendment that would be passed to allow both African American men and women the right to vote. Others, however, disagreed. They understood that, with the momentum brought about by the North's victory, the Senate was on the cusp of giving suffrage to African American men—and there wasn't the same level of support within Washington to give women the right to vote. Because of this, some women's rights advocates and abolitionists, including Lucy Stone and Frederick Douglass, believed that it was silly to wait out for universal suffrage when the right to vote for African American men could be won without delay.

Frederick Douglass, in a famous speech, referred to the many riots that were taking place in the South after the Civil War, in which African American men were killed and lynched by white mobs. "When women, because they are women … are dragged from their houses and are hung from lampposts; when their children are torn from their arms, and their brains bashed out upon the pavement … then they will have an urgency to obtain the ballot equal to our own," he told the crowd.[2] Douglass felt African American men needed the right to vote for representatives and laws that would protect them. After African American men got the right to vote, Douglass argued, it would be the turn of women.

Susan B. Anthony and Elizabeth Cady Stanton spoke out against the passage of the Fifteenth Amendment. They believed that giving African American men the right to vote before women would create an "aristocracy of sex," in which all men had power over all women.[3] Lucy Stone, however, believed women's suffrage would be passed soon enough.

In 1869, the American Equal Rights Foundation (AERA), an organization that campaigned for universal suffrage, broke up over these disagreements. Stanton, Anthony, and their allies formed the National Woman Suffrage Association (NWSA), while Lucy Stone and her allies formed the American Woman Suffrage Association (AWSA). These groups remained separated for almost thirty years.

The Fifteenth Amendment was ratified in 1870. It states, "The right of citizens of the United States to vote shall not be denied or abridged by the United States or by any State on account of race, color, or previous condition of servitude."[4]

The Nineteenth Amendment

While advocates like Lucy Stone hoped that women's suffrage would come soon after the passage of the Fifteenth Amendment, they were wrong.

The Founding Mothers of the women's suffrage movement would die before they saw the realization of their dreams. The Nineteenth Amendment was ratified on August 18, 1920, nearly eighty years after the Seneca Falls Convention. The next step was ratification by a three-fourths majority of

Racism Within the Movement

The fight for women's suffrage was an important moment within the United States for women. But it was not without its problems. In the 1960s, feminist scholars like Angela Davis noted how women's suffrage fought for rights of wealthy, white women, and no others. For example, Elizabeth Cady Stanton used racist language to argue why African Americans were not as deserving of political rights and representation as white women were. This is the difficult history of first-wave feminism that would form a major part of second-wave feminism nearly one hundred years later.

Lucy Stone believed that once all men had the vote, it would be given to women soon after. She was to be proven wrong. Stone was the first woman to graduate from college in Massachusetts.

all the states, which was thirty-six states. By the spring of 1920, thirty-five states had ratified the bill.

Most of the southern states declared their opposition to the bill, with one state remaining: Tennessee. Tennessee legislators were torn over the issue of the bill, with forty-eight representatives for its passage and forty-eight against.

The tiebreaking vote would fall to twenty-three-year-old representative Harry T. Burn. At first, Burn was opposed to the amendment. But with his mother's convincing, he agreed to vote for it. With his vote, the Nineteenth Amendment would become law.

The Nineteenth Amendment, enshrined in the US Constitution, reads: "The right of citizens of the United States to vote shall not be denied or abridged by the United States or by any State on account of sex."[5]

The Equal Rights Amendment and Second-Wave Feminism

With the passage of the Nineteenth Amendment, women suffragists were briefly satisfied. However, this would not last very long. For many women, national suffrage was but the first step. The Nineteenth Amendment guaranteed female citizens a say in the governance of their country, but it did not provide them with equal rights. For women's rights activists, equal legal footing was the only acceptable next step in the movement.

Explicit Equality

Beginning in 1921, Alice Paul, the head of the National Woman's Party, began to work on a new amendment to the Constitution that would specifically address equal rights regardless of sex. The first draft of this amendment read, in part: "No political, civil, or legal disabilities or inequalities on account of sex or on account of marriage, unless applying equally to both sexes, shall exist within the United States or any territory subject to the jurisdiction thereof."

In 1923, Paul further revised this amendment. It read: "Men and women shall have equal rights throughout the United States and every place subject to its jurisdiction. Congress shall have power to enforce this article by appropriate legislation."[1] Paul called this proposed amendment the Lucretia Mott Amendment, after the famous suffragist and abolitionist, and began to advocate for its passage.

Women picket at the White House in 1917, demanding the right to vote. Even after women won that right a few years later, their fight for equal rights would continue.

Alice Paul, the head of the National Woman's Party, stands in front of a women's suffrage flag that she sewed.

There was still disagreement about what equal rights meant specifi-cally for American women. Paul believed that full equality was essential to women's rights, even if it meant that women would not be able to keep certain benefits that had been granted to them based on their sex, such as no night work or heavy lifting at work, and if they would be eligible for the military draft. Other women's rights advocates voiced their opinion that women had different experiences than men and complete legal equality would not work. These advocates argued that women were still the primary caretakers of their families—meaning that some sex-based labor protec-tions should still exist. Also, these critics argued, women needed special laws for maternity leave that men did not need.

The Equal Rights Amendment, as the Lucretia Mott Amendment came to be known, was introduced into committee in Congress in the fall of 1921. However, it did not receive enough votes to go to the floor of the House of Representatives or the Senate. In 1946, the ERA reached the floor of the Senate, only to be blocked by a vote of thirty-eight to thirty-five.[2] Although the bill received the majority votes, it could not pass the Senate because amendments need a two-thirds supermajority.

The Stop ERA Campaign

As the ERA was gaining steam in 1973, public support began to wane. This was largely due to the influence of the Stop ERA Campaign, led by Phyllis Schlafly.

Schlafly argued that the passage of the ERA would upend traditional male and female roles in the United States. She stoked fears by arguing that women would soon be called to serve in the military during times of war as part of the draft. She also declared that women would be less likely to receive custody of their children in the circumstance of divorce if the ERA was passed.[3]

THE EQUAL RIGHTS AMENDMENT AND SECOND-WAVE FEMINISM

With the emergence of second-wave feminism in the 1960s and 1970s, the ERA once again became a goal for feminists. Second-wave feminism, unlike first-wave feminism, focused not solely on women's right to vote but other protections that were not guaranteed to women under the Constitution—especially the right of women to pursue careers and passions outside of the home. As part of this movement, the Equal Rights Amendment was rewritten. Its new aim was to "even the playing field" for women, including introducing reproductive and employment rights for women under both federal and state laws.

Phyllis Schlafly led an anti-ERA movement, fearing that traditional roles of men and women would be forever changed by its passage.

A Debate Over Difference

Second-wave feminist leaders Gloria Steinem and Dorothy Pitman-Hughes championed the ERA. Others argued that the ERA was not a solution because women *are* different from men. These people argued that women do not need legal equality on the federal level but, instead, individual legal protections.

The debate over whether women were inherently different from men raged on throughout the 1960s and 1970s. Throughout much of the 1960s, the ERA was largely tabled in the interest of ending racial segregation. The Civil Rights Act was passed in 1964—with the explicit prohibition of discrimination based on sex as well as race, which was seen as a small victory for women's rights.

In 1972, the ERA once again passed the US Senate and was sent to the states for ratification. Over the course of a year, thirty-one states ratified what would have become the Twenty-Seventh Amendment. With a large conservative backlash in the mid-1970s, however, support for the amendment waned. It was unable to reach ratification by thirty-eight states, or three-fourths of the states in the union, to become law.

The ERA has still not been passed. It now reads, "Equality of rights under the law shall not be abridged by the United States or by any State on account of sex."[4] There is still no mention of equal rights based on sex in the Constitution.

5

Where We Are Today

Much has changed since that hot and humid day in July 1848 when women gathered and demanded equal rights under the Constitution of the United States. While women have been able to vote in the United States for nearly one hundred years, there are still no explicit protections for women within the US Constitution. Many women continue to fight for the ratification of the ERA and for other protections over their bodies, in the workforce, and in politics. It is a long battle, and one with no quick solution.

Important Steps Forward

In the summer of 1993, representatives from countries all around the world flocked to Vienna, Austria, for the largest human rights conference ever organized. During the World Conference on Human Rights, which was organized by the United Nations (UN), representatives spoke a lot about women's rights in particular. Human rights workers have long recognized that women are more likely than men to be victims of violence and sexual attacks.

They are also more likely to face poverty. The American politician and feminist Geraldine Ferraro wrote about the situation across the globe: "When little girls get less food, less medical care, less education and more work than little boys; when women can't travel, marry or leave home without some man's permission; when rights to vote, meet and speak out are circumscribed; when children and property belong legally only to men; when women are denied the right to control their bodies, how can women be fully human?"[1]

The UN had previously taken action on the status of women across the globe with the Convention on the Elimination of All Forms of Discrimination Against Women (CEDAW), which was adopted in 1979. CEDAW stated that nations that signed the agreement would take all necessary steps to abolish any laws that discriminated against women and that all women should have equal access to education, voting and property rights, and health care. More than 180 countries signed CEDAW. (In fact, the only industrialized Western country that hasn't signed it is the United States, which has led many critics to question whether the United States has prioritized women's rights.)[2] But, while CEDAW was an important step forward, many people, like Ferraro, argued that more steps needed to be taken. Women still did not have equal footing to men. And, most concerning, violence against women was still a significant problem across the globe.

Representatives at the Vienna Conference soon decided that widespread violence against women was a problem and that it was time to take additional action. In December of that year, the UN passed the Declaration on the Elimination of Violence Against Women. This resolution stated "the urgent need for the universal application to women of the rights and principles with regard to equality, security, liberty, integrity and dignity of all human beings." The continued inequality of women across the globe was once again gaining worldwide attention.

Geraldine Ferraro was the first female vice presidential candidate for either political party, in 1984.

In the United States, the call for more legal protections for women was gaining more traction, too. On September 13, 1994, President Bill Clinton signed the Violence Against Women Act (VAWA). This was an important moment in the history of women's rights. It was the first federal law that addressed the issue of violence against women. This act provided a good amount of funding toward investigating violent crimes against women. It also established the Office on Violence Against Women, which acted within the US Department of Justice.[3]

Since its passage, the VAWA has improved the federal government's ability to investigate and prosecute violence against women, and to provide services for victims of such violent crime. It has made stalking illegal, has restricted states from making women pay for medical tests after sexual

President Barack Obama signs the Lilly Ledbetter Act into law, an act that aims to close the pay gap between men and women.

assaults, and has provided education and training programs for health care providers and law enforcement officers.

The Debate Rages On

Women's rights and constitutional protections remain debated today. More than ever before, women play a larger role in the workplace, with most women working outside of the home—even as they are raising families. Yet women still earn less than men in the same professions—on average seventy-seven cents to every dollar that a man earns.[4]

In 1963, President John F. Kennedy signed the Equal Pay Act into law, which stated that two employees at the same company who did the same work needed to receive equal pay, regardless of their gender. However, this act only referred to base pay and did not take into account merit pay, bonuses, or other forms of payment.

The Lilly Ledbetter Act, signed into law by President Barack Obama in 2009, aimed to close this gap and to provide equal pay for women and men. Under this act, employers must pay their employees equally, regardless of gender, and employees have the right to challenge unfair pay even if they are not aware of pay differences at the time of their employment. For many feminists, this was an important step—although it was a step short of passing the ERA.

The Era of the ERA?

Several movements have reignited interest in the ERA and women's constitutional rights. They include the Women's March on Washington, following the election of Donald Trump in 2016, and the Me Too movement (#MeToo) in 2017. These movements have made public important discussions on consent, women's rights over their own bodies, and protections in the workplace for women. For the first time, the extent of injustices that women experience in daily life is becoming discussed in public and political life. The publicity of the #MeToo movement has highlighted why women need additional protections in the workforce. It has shown that women still are frequent victims of sexual violence in the workplace and that they often are unheard when they report these violations. Many women have kept silent about abuse for decades, afraid that they would be ridiculed or ignored by the public and by law enforcement. But times are changing. For the first time, the general public and law enforcement are listening to the voices of these women. The long-term effects of the #MeToo movement in protecting women against sexual violence remain to be seen.

The fate of the ERA is also still unknown. On March 22, 2017, Nevada became the thirty-sixth state to ratify the ERA, nearly forty-five years after the bill was first sent to the states for ratification. On May 30, 2018, Illinois became the thirty-seventh state to vote to ratify the ERA.[5] This means that the ERA is only one state short of the three-fourths majority of states required for the passage of an amendment. Although the deadline for ratification of the states passed in 1982, many legal scholars believe that if thirty-eight states show their support for the ERA, the deadline can be shifted and the bill might have a chance of becoming ratified as an amendment to the United States Constitution.[6]

What Comes Next?

Will the ERA have enough support in the divided political climate to get passed? Will the #MeToo movement solidify women's protections or divide debate over gender-based rights?

The answers to these questions have yet to be found, but the open discussion over women's rights in the workforce and at home is an important step forward. It is the first step in recognizing that the history of inequality for women in the United States—and within larger society—is long and dark.

#MeToo

The #MeToo movement began in October 2017, with women across social media using the hashtag #MeToo to address the sexual harassment from men that they experienced in their lives. This movement was largely based on the work of activist Tarana Burke, who began using the phrase "me too" to empower women, and especially women of color, to talk about sexual abuse by sharing their own experiences. #MeToo activists have argued for more protections for women and non-gender conforming individuals in the workplace and beyond—a central tenant of the ERA.

The road goes ever on. The Women's March in January 2017 showed that women remain committed to fighting for equal rights, equal pay, and equal say in the future of the United States.

Women were only granted the right to vote one hundred years ago. Their voices are only now being more widely heard in terms of sexual abuse. But that doesn't mean it is where the fight for women's rights will remain. The Constitution enshrined new rights for groups of citizens that did not have those freedoms before. Over the past two hundred years, the Constitution has been amended to reflect new rights, freedoms, and values. It is a living and breathing document that can—and will—change to ensure a brighter future for all of its citizens.

Chapter Notes

Introduction

1. "Get Statistics," National Sexual Violence Resource Center, https://www.nsvrc.org/statistics.

2. "All Amendments to the United States Constitution," University of Minnesota: Human Rights Library, http://hrlibrary.umn.edu/education/all_amendments_usconst.htm.

Chapter 1. The Creation of the Constitution

1. "Delegates of the Continental Congress Who Signed the United States Constitution," History, Art and Archives: The United States House of Representatives, https://history.house.gov/People/Signatories/Signatories.

2. "Madison Debates September 17," The Avalon Project: Documents in Law, History and Diplomacy, Yale Law School: Lillian Goldman Law Library, 2008, http://avalon.law.yale.edu/18th_century/debates_917.asp.

3. Mercy Otis Warren, "Observations on the New Constitution, and on the Federal and State Conventions," Constitution.org, 1788, https://www.constitution.org/cmt/mowarren/observations_new_constitution_1788.html.

4. Abigail Adams, "Letter from Abigail Adams to John Adams, 31 March – 5 April 1776," Adams Family Papers: An Electronic Archive, Massachusetts Historical Society, https://www.masshist.org/digitaladams/archive/doc?id=L17760331aa.

Chapter 2. The Early Women's Rights Movement

1. Frederick Douglass, "(1888) Frederick Douglass on Woman Suffrage," From *Woman's Journal*, April 14, 1888, Blackpast.org, https://blackpast.org/1888-frederick-douglass-woman-suffrage.

2. Horace Seldon, "A Life of Purpose," The Liberator Files, http://theliberatorfiles.com/a-portrait-of-purpose.

3. "Seneca Falls Convention," History.com, November 10, 2017, https://www.history.com/topics/womens-rights/seneca-falls-convention.

4. Sojourner Truth, "Aint I a Woman?," National Park Service, November 17, 2017, https://www.nps.gov/articles/sojourner-truth.htm.

5. *The North Star,* Frederick Douglass, July 28, 1878, http://utc.iath.virginia.edu/abolitn/abwm03dt.html.

6. Frederick Douglass, "The Rights of Women," *The North Star*, July 28, 1848, From Uncle Tom's Cabin and American Culture: A Multi-Media Archive, the University of Virginia, http://ecssba.rutgers.edu/docs/seneca.html.

Chapter 3. Amendments to the Constitution

1. "14th and 15th Amendments," National Women's History Museum, http://www.crusadeforthevote.org/14-15-amendments.

2. Adam Gopnik, "A Critic at Large: American Prophet: The Gifts of Frederick Douglass," *New Yorker*, October 15, 2018.

3. Susan B. Anthony, "The Aristocracy of Sex—A Note from Miss Susan B Anthony," *New York Times*, June 5, 1869, https://www.nytimes.com/1869/06/05/archives/the-aristocracy-of-sexnote-from-miss-susan-b-anthony.html.

4. "15th Amendment to the U.S. Constitution," Primary Documents in American History, The Library of Congress, https://www.loc.gov/rr/program/bib/ourdocs/15thamendment.html.

5. Nancy Gertner and Gail Heriot, "The Nineteenth Amendment," Constitution Center, https://constitutioncenter.org/interactive-constitution/amendments/amendment-xix.

Chapter 4. The Equal Rights Amendment and Second-Wave Feminism

1. Roberta W. Francis, "The History Behind the Equal Rights Amendment," The Equal Rights Amendment: Unfinished Business for the Constitution, https://www.equalrightsamendment.org/history.htm.

2. "Frequently Asked Questions," The Equal Rights Amendment: Unfinished Business for the Constitution, https://www.equalrightsamendment.org/faq.htm#q3.

3. Nadeem Muaddi, "10 Quotes that Define Phyllis Schlafly's Life as an Anti-Feminist," CNN, September 6, 2016, https://www.cnn.com/2016/09/06/politics/phyllis-schlafly-quotes/index.html.

4. "The Equal Rights Amendment," The Equal Rights Amendment: Unfinished Business for the Constitution, https://www.equalrightsamendment.org.

Chapter 5. Where We Are Today

1. Geraldine Ferraro, "Human Rights for Women," New York Times, June 10, 1993, https://www.nytimes.com/1993/06/10/opinion/human-rights-for-women.html.

2. Linda Napikoski, "A Brief History of CEDAW," ThoughtCo, March 6, 2017, https://www.thoughtco.com/brief-history-of-cedaw-3529470.

3. "History of the Violence Against Women Act," Legal Momentum, https://www.legalmomentum.org/history-vawa.

4. Louis Jacobson, "Barack Obama, in State of the Union, Says Women Make 77 Cents for Every Dollar a Man Earns," Politifact, January 29, 2014, https://www.politifact.com/truth-o-meter/statements/2014/jan/29/barack-obama/barack-obama-state-union-says-women-make-77-cents.

5. "The ERA in the States," The Equal Rights Amendment: Unfinished Business for the Constitution, https://www.equalrightsamendment.org/states.htm.

6. Matthew Haag, "The Equal Rights Amendment Was Just Ratified by Illinois. What Does That Mean?," May 31, 2018, https://www.nytimes.com/2018/05/31/us/equal-rights-amendment-illinois.html.

Glossary

abolitionist A person who works to abolish or end an institution, such as slavery.

amendment An article added to the US Constitution; a change to a document.

coerced To be persuaded or forced to do something.

coverture The legal status of married women, meaning that she was under her husband's protection and authority and she had no financial rights of her own.

delegate A person sent to represent other citizens during a political process.

Dower Rights An outdated law by which a wife could gain control of property and finances after the death of her husband.

Enlightenment A European philosophical movement during the late seventeenth and early eighteenth centuries that emphasized reason and individuality over tradition.

exclusionary Relating to the exclusion of something or someone.

federal Relating to the central government that governs over multiple states and jurisdictions.

feminism The belief that women are equal to men and should be treated as such.

intersectionality The intersection, or interconnectedness, of different characteristics, such as sex, gender, race, or religion.

ratification Signing or giving consent to an agreement or a bill, to make it law.

suffrage The right to vote in elections.

supermajority A number that is larger than half the total, particularly used in political votes.

Further Reading

Books

Conkling, Winifred. *Votes for Women!: American Suffragists and the Battle for the Ballot*. Chapel Hill, NC: Algonquin Young Readers, 2018.

Hurt, Avery Elizabeth. *Feminism*. New York, NY: Greenhaven Publishing, 2019.

Kops, Deborah. *Alice Paul and the Fight for Women's Rights: From the Vote to the Equal Rights Amendment*. Honesdale, PA: Calkins Creek, 2017.

Lynch, Seth. *Women's Suffrage*. New York, NY: Gareth Stevens Publishing, 2019.

Zimet, Susan. *Roses and Radicals: The Epic Story of How American Women Won the Right to Vote*. New York, NY: Viking Books for Young Readers, 2018.

Websites

The Equal Rights Amendment (ERA)
www.equalrightsamendment.org
The official website for the Equal Rights Amendment provides the history of the bill, as well as resources, including videos and other media.

The Library of Congress (LOC)
www.loc.gov/collections/national-american-woman-suffrage-association/about-this-collection
This Library of Congress collection offers full-text digital copies of many important texts of the women's rights movement, including the Declaration of Sentiments.

The National Organization for Women (NOW)
now.org
The official website of the National Organization for Women provides resources about women's rights in the United States, including the advancement of voting rights for women and the passage of the ERA.

Index